CHECKERBOARD HOW-TO LIBRARY

COOL CRAFTS

Cool Rubber Stamp Art

Pam Price

ABDO
Publishing Company

visit us at
www.abdopub.com

Published by ABDO Publishing Company, 4940 Viking Drive, Edina, Minnesota 55435. Copyright © 2005 by Abdo Consulting Group, Inc. International copyrights reserved in all countries. No part of this book may be reproduced in any form without written permission from the publisher. Checkerboard Library is a trademark and logo of ABDO Publishing Company.

Printed in the United States.

Design and Production: Mighty Media, Inc.
Cover Photo: Anders Hanson
Interior Photos: Anders Hanson
Series Coordinator: Pam Scheunemann
Art Direction: Pam Scheunemann

Library of Congress Cataloging-in-Publication Data

Price, Pamela S.
Cool rubber stamp art / Pam Price.
p. cm. -- (Cool crafts)
ISBN 1-59197-743-6
1. Rubber stamp printing--Juvenile literature. 2. Rubber stamp art--Juvenile literature. I. Title. II. Series.

TT867.p75 2004
761--dc22

2004053123

Commercial art stamps featured in this book are copyright and used with permission from A Stamp in the Hand; Bizzaro; Fred B. Mullett, Stamps from Nature Prints; Hero Arts; JudiKins; Magenta; Om Studio; Duncan Enterprises/PSX Design For Creativity; Stampabilities; Stamp Francisco; The Artful Stamper.

For Your Safety
Some of the tools shown in this book should be used only when an adult is present.

J-Nf   3 9547 00272 6458

Contents

Boldfaced words throughout the text are defined in the glossary.

Introduction

Much of the history of stamping revolves around legal issues. In the days when few people knew how to write, they would dictate letters to **scribes**. The person who hired the scribe would stamp his seal on the document to authenticate it. This also let others know that the contents were important. These seals were unique, intricate, and therefore hard to duplicate.

Over time, people began to seal documents with soft wax. They would **impress** their seal into the wax. People who had to seal and authenticate a lot of documents wore **signet rings** containing such seals. These seals also protected the privacy of documents. If the seal was broken, you knew someone had read the document.

Seals are still used today in China and Japan. The seals they use are called chops. Artists often use them to sign and identify their work.

When postage stamps were introduced in the United States in 1847, they were quite expensive. The government required postmasters to damage the stamps to prevent people from reusing them. They called this canceling the stamp. Some did this by writing on the stamps. But it was time-consuming to write on every single stamp that passed through a post office.

Soon, many postmasters made stamps they could use to cancel the stamps. They would carve a design into the end of a cork, dip it in ink, then press it over the stamp. Eventually, metal hand stamps that were uniform in design replaced the homemade cork stamps. These in turn were replaced by rubber stamps.

Eventually, people used stamping as a way of recording images found in nature. They would coat leaves and flowers with ink and press them onto paper. They would study these **impressions** and share them with other people.

In the 1860s, Japanese fishermen began making impressions of the prize fish they caught. The fisherman would cover the fish with ink and then lay rice paper over it to make the impression. This practice is called *gyotaku*, which means "fish impression" in Japanese. Gyotaku is still practiced today.

The craft of stamping as we practice it today become popular in the 1980s. Then, the craft was pretty basic. **Embossing** a stamped image was about as fancy as stamping got. Since then, however, new materials, techniques, and tools have been developed.

In this book we will introduce you to the basic tools and techniques of rubber stamping. We'll also show you how to stamp cards, gift wrap, tote bags, and even flowerpots. Once you learn the basic techniques, set your imagination free! You'll find there are all kinds of cool things you can stamp.

Stamps, Ink & Paper

It is relatively inexpensive to get started in rubber stamping. The expense comes as you start acquiring more stamps and tools. One great way to keep the cost down is to share stamps and inks with your friends.

Stamps

Stamps are the heart of rubber stamping. **Commercial** stamps are fun, but don't rule out homemade stamps, sponges, and even fruit.

Commercial stamps are the stamps you find in craft stores, on the Internet, and in catalogs. They come in almost any style and design you can think of.

Homemade

Homemade stamps can be carved from just about anything you can imagine. You can make them from linoleum cuts, woodcuts, corks, and potatoes.

Found objects

Found objects are just that, objects that you find. Try stamping with leaves and flowers. Or, make cool prints with apples, star fruits, and mushrooms.

Taking Care of Your Rubber Stamps

Store your stamps rubber side down in a cool, dark, dry location. Avoid storing stamps in heat or direct sunlight. This will cause the rubber to become brittle.

Clean your stamps each time you use them. Place a pad of paper towels dampened with window cleaner on a plate. Pounce your stamp on the damp paper towels and then on a dry paper towel.

You can also use stamp cleaner to clean your stamps. An old, soft toothbrush is helpful if the stamp is really a mess. Never dunk a stamp mounted on a wood block in water. It can loosen the bond between the rubber and the cushion layer.

Ink Pads

There are many colors and types of ink pads. Most stampers have one pad with black dye ink and several different colors of **pigment** ink pads. Choose raised ink pads with removable covers. These allow you to easily ink a stamp that is larger than the pad.

Pigment ink

Pigment inks have vibrant colors that are fade resistant and long lasting. Pigment ink takes a long time to dry. So, be careful not to smear your images when working with it. It won't dry at all on coated, glossy paper. If you use pigment ink on glossy paper, you must **emboss** the image.
Pigment ink cleans up with water.

Archival ink

Archival means that the ink is free of acid and won't harm the paper. Scrapbookers use archival-quality inks and papers so their scrapbook pages won't deteriorate over time.

Water-based dye ink

Dye ink is water based and fast drying. It will dry on coated, glossy paper. However, do not use dye ink if you plan to watercolor the images. Dye ink will run when it gets wet! Dye ink is not good for **embossing** because it dries so quickly. Dye ink cleans up with water.

Dye-based ink

Dye-based ink is not permanent, but it is waterproof. This is a good ink to use if you plan to use watercolor paints or markers to color the image later. It may not dry completely on some glossy papers. Use a **solvent**-based cleaner to clean dye-based ink from your stamps.

Permanent ink

Permanent ink is waterproof. It is good for stamping on ceramics, glass, plastic, terra-cotta, glossy paper, polymer clay, metal, and wood. Most permanent inks are solvent based. There are some water-based permanent inks, though. You will have to use stamp cleaner to clean permanent ink off your stamps.

Rainbow ink pads

Rainbow ink pads contain several colors of ink in one pad. Be careful when inking your stamps not to get ink from one pad on the one next to it.

Mini stamp pads

Mini stamp pads are useful for inking up small stamps. They are also great if you want to print just one part of a stamp and not the whole thing.

Fabric and craft ink

To make fabric ink permanent, you must heat set it. This can be done with an iron or a heat gun. Get an adult to do this.

> **Tip**
> Store your ink pads upside down so the ink settles to the top surface. This gives you a nice, wet surface for inking up your stamps.

Paper

Make sure you match your paper to your ink. **Pigment** inks won't dry on glossy papers. Dye inks will spread in papers that are really absorbent. Here are some of the types of papers you may want to experiment with.

Cardstock

Cardstock is a heavyweight paper used for making greeting cards and gift tags. It is available in many colors and patterns.

Decorative paper

Decorative paper is available in many colors, patterns, and themes. You can stamp on these or use them for matting images you've stamped on plain paper.

Vellum

Vellum is a thin, transparent paper. It comes in white or colors. You can stamp on the vellum or layer it over an image you've stamped.

Craft paper

Craft paper comes in rolls. It comes in white and several shades of brown. Use craft paper to make your own wrapping paper!

Bags

Most craft stores carry brown, white, and colored paper bags for making custom gift bags. For canvas tote bags, look at office supply stores, fabric stores, and craft stores.

Tip

If you don't like what you stamped with your fabric ink, don't heat set it. Wash it and the image will come out so you can try again.

Other Tools & Materials

While stamps, ink, and paper will get you started, you'll need some of these tools and materials to stamp on surfaces other than paper. You'll also use these items to **embellish** your projects.

Markers, Pens, and Pencils

You can use pens and colored pencils to color your stamped images. Markers are handy for inking a stamp and for coloring stamped images.

Markers

Color your stamp with markers to make a multicolored image. Or use them to color images after you stamp them. But use waterproof ink if you do this!

Gel pens and metallic pens

Gel and metallic inks look really dramatic on dark-colored and black paper.

Fabric pens

Use fabric pens for coloring images stamped on fabric.

Colored pencils

Use colored pencils to color stamped images. Watercolor pencils can be blended with a wet paintbrush after coloring. However, make sure you stamp the image in waterproof ink or it will run.

Paint

For some projects, you might want to use paint instead of ink. It works best with stamps that don't have a lot of fine detail. Surfaces on which you might want to use paint include wood, clay, walls, and fabric.

Acrylic paint

Use acrylic paint for stamping on paper, fabric, wood, terra-cotta, and more. Acrylics come in jars, bottles, and tubes. You can apply it to a stamp with a brush, sponge, or brayer. Acrylic paints clean up with water.

Watercolor paint

You can use watercolor paints on paper and fabric. Watercolor paints come in tubes and in trays called pans. To use pan paints, just run a wet brush over the surface of the block of paint. Thin watercolor paints that come in tubes with water before you paint with them.

You can also use watercolors to paint stamped images. Be sure to stamp with waterproof ink so the image doesn't run when you paint it. You can also paint a background and then stamp on it when it dries.

Fabric paint

Fabric paint is usually water based. It must be heat set to make the image permanent. Many acrylic craft paints can also be used on fabric.

Tools

Stamps, ink, and paper are all you really need to get started with rubber stamping. These additional tools will help you **embellish** your projects.

Brayers

Use a sponge brayer to make textured backgrounds. Use a soft rubber brayer to ink up stamps or roll out backgrounds.

Sponges

Sponges are great for stamping. Get a variety of textures and sizes for different uses. Use sea sponges for making textured backgrounds with ink or paint. Makeup sponges are good for dabbing paint onto stamps and for blending watercolors. Use pop-up sponges to make your own sponge stamps.

Paintbrushes

Choose medium-quality synthetic-bristle brushes made for painting with acrylic paints. Use a brush with a fine tip for coloring detailed areas of images. Use broader tips for blending colors and painting backgrounds. Keep your brushes in a glass of water while you're working and clean them right away when you're finished. If acrylic paint dries in the brush, it is very hard to get out.

Tip
Plastic plates make great disposable painter's palettes.

Scissors and trimmers

You will need regular paper scissors for cutting paper to size. Decorative-edge scissors have blades that cut a pattern into paper. They're nice for making decorative edges on greeting cards. Use nail scissors or embroidery scissors for detailed cutting, such as cutting out a stamped image.

If you do a lot of paper crafts, consider buying a small paper trimmer. It's really easy to trim paper to size and make straight cuts with a paper trimmer.

Embellishments

Embellishments are things you add to your project to decorate it. Common embellishments include

- Glitter
- **Eyelets**
- Charms
- Buttons

Adhesives

You will need several types of adhesive for your rubber stamping projects. Use double-stick photo tape to layer elements. Use foam spacer tape between layers to create the impression of depth. Glue pens are handy for gluing on glitter, charms, and buttons.

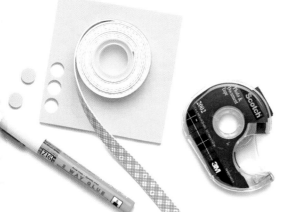

Basic Techniques

Rubber stamping really is pretty easy. You just **pounce** the stamp on the ink pad a few times. Then you press the stamp onto whatever you're stamping. However, there are a few techniques that will help you make the best possible images.

Pounce the stamp straight up and down when inking it.

Not enough ink

Too much ink

Just right

Inking the Stamp

Always use a clean stamp so you don't ruin your ink pad. Press the stamp lightly several times on the ink pad. Don't twist the stamp on the pad. That only wears out the pad. Do turn the stamp each time you lift it. That gives more even ink coverage. Even ink coverage on the stamp means your image won't be light in some places and dark in others.

Don't over-ink the stamp or you'll clog the stamp and lose detail in the image. Avoid rocking the stamp back and forth on the ink pad. That applies the ink unevenly and gets ink on the edges of the stamp.

When inking large stamps, you'll find it easiest to lay the stamp rubber side up and gently press the ink pad onto the stamp.

Making a Good Impression

Position the stamp over the paper and set it straight down. If your stamp is small, press down evenly on it with your fingertips. If the stamp is large, place your palm on the stamp and apply light, even pressure to the stamp.

Now grasp the edges of the stamp and lift straight up. If the paper sticks to the wet ink on the stamp, gently hold the paper down while you lift off the stamp.

Avoid rocking the stamp back and forth. That makes smeary lines. And, if you got any ink on the stamp edges when you inked it, rocking may get some of that ink on the paper.

Reink the stamp before you stamp again. Otherwise, the second image will be lighter than the first image.

Lay large stamps on the table to ink them.

Press small stamps evenly with the fingertips.

Press large stamps evenly with the palm.

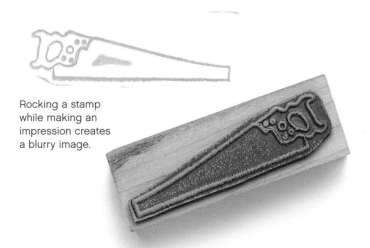

Rocking a stamp while making an impression creates a blurry image.

Creative Techniques

Here's where the really creative part of rubber stamping happens. Decorate your stamped images with paint and markers. Make cool backgrounds. Create the illusion of a three-dimensional image by layering. **Emboss** an image for a blast of color and texture.

Stamping with Markers

Use this technique to print a multicolored image. Choose the colors you want for the different areas of the image. Then, working quickly, ink the stamp. If the marker ink dries before you can print your image, breathe a quick, hard blast of air on it to rewet the ink.

Stamping with Paint

This technique is best with stamps that don't have a lot of fine detail. Pour some paint onto a plate. Dip a makeup sponge into the paint and **pounce** it on the plate to remove the excess paint.

Now use the sponge to dab paint evenly onto the stamp. Be sure to practice on scrap paper until you get the technique down. A blurry image means you applied too much paint. A faint image means you didn't use enough paint.

Pounce off excess paint before dabbing paint on the stamp.

Not enough paint   Just right

Too much paint

Creating a Background

Backgrounds add a lot to a stamped image. Choose a lighter color for your background so it doesn't **detract** from your images. You can use a stamp, a brayer, a brush, or a sponge to create a background.

Stamped backgrounds

There are special stamps made for creating backgrounds. They have no detail, just a shape. They often have a decorative edge. Simply ink up the stamp and press it onto the paper.

Backgrounds made with brayers

Use a sponge brayer to create a textured background. Use a soft rubber brayer to make a smooth-looking background. Simply roll the brayer through the ink or paint and roll it onto the paper.

soft rubber brayer   foam brayer

Sponged backgrounds

Dip a piece of sea sponge into watercolor paint and lightly **pounce** it across your paper. Space out the sponge marks if you use more than one color. A multicolor background looks better if you don't entirely cover the paper with each color.

Layering

You can create the illusion of a three-dimensional image by stamping an image twice and layering them. Stamp the image first on whatever you are making. Then stamp it again on a scrap of the same paper. Cut out the image you made on the scrap and mount it above the first image with spacer tape.

Coloring Stamped Images

After stamping images, you can color them with colored pencils, markers, or watercolor paints. Be sure to stamp with waterproof ink if you will be using water-based markers or watercolor paints. Otherwise the image will run when you color it.

For a softer look, color with water-based markers. Then use a damp paintbrush to go over it. This will make it look more like a watercolor painting.

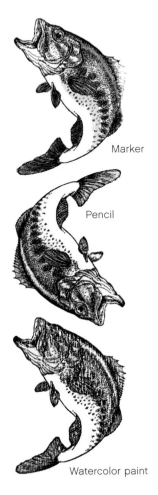

Marker

Pencil

Watercolor paint

Heat Embossing

An **embossed** image is raised. Embossing powder is made up of very small plastic pellets that melt when you apply heat to them. You have to use a heat gun to get the plastic hot enough to melt. Although a heat gun looks like a hair drier, it gets much, much hotter. You need an adult to do this part of the embossing for you.

To emboss an image, pour embossing powder on the image while the ink is still wet. Pour the embossing powder that doesn't stick back into the container. Now have your adult helper hold the heat gun a couple of inches above the image until the powder melts and rises.

Caution!
Heat guns quickly get to 700 degrees (371°C). Do not use a heat gun yourself. You could burn yourself badly or start a fire. Always have an adult use the heat gun.

Embellishments

When you **embellish** something, you decorate it. An embellishment could be a leaf, a ribbon, a die cut, a button, or a charm.

Most embellishments can simply be glued on. The hardest part is not attaching them, but deciding what to use and where to put it. Remember that sometimes less is more. Don't add so much stuff to your project that it **detracts** from your **focal point**. The point of adding embellishments is simply to accent your stamping.

Eyelets

One embellishment that takes a bit more work to add is **eyelets**. You will need some special tools in addition to the eyelets. These are a pounding mat, a punch, an eyelet setting tool, and a small hammer.

To attach an eyelet, first use the punch to make a small hole where you want to place the eyelet. Put the eyelet in the hole and carefully turn the paper facedown. Place the setting tool in the end of the eyelet. Now tap the end of the setting tool firmly with the hammer. Continue tapping until the end of the eyelet flares out and the eyelet is securely fastened.

If you are putting an eyelet through two layers of paper, put double-stick tape between the layers to keep them from slipping out of position while you work.

Tap the eyelet tool until the eyelet flares out.

Terra-Cotta Flowerpot

Terra-cotta flowerpots have many uses. You can store combs and brushes in them. You can use them as pencil jars. You can put candles in them. You can even put plants in them! You can buy terra-cotta flowerpots at garden centers and at craft stores.

What You Need

- Terra-cotta flowerpot and saucer
- Latex house paint
- Paintbrush
- Foam sanding sponge
- Acrylic paints
- Plastic plates
- Makeup sponges or foam craft sponges
- Daisy rubber stamp

1 Paint the flowerpot and saucer with latex house paint. Let the paint dry overnight. Lightly sand the edges of the flowerpot so the terra-cotta shows through the paint. Wipe off all the dust.

2 Pour some paint onto a disposable plate. Dip a sponge in the paint and **pounce** off the excess paint. Dab paint on the stamp. We used orange for the center of the daisy and white for the petals.

3 Because the flowerpot curves, you have to use a rolling motion when stamping. Set one edge of the stamp on the flowerpot, then roll it along the pot. Lift the stamp straight off of the flowerpot.

4 Along the edges of the flowerpot, place the stamp so only half of the stamp is on the flowerpot. Use a paintbrush to touch up any daisies that have bare spots. Or, if you like them, leave the bare spots!

Spring Greeting Card

This cheerful greeting card is accented with layering and color highlights. Use this card as a birthday card or a Mother's Day card. Or, give it to a friend just to say hello.

What You Need

- Yellow cardstock trimmed to 6½ by 9½ inches (17 by 24 cm)
- White cardstock trimmed to 3 by 5½ inches (8 by 14 cm)
- Scrap of white cardstock
- Tulip stamp
- Bumblebee stamp
- Red and green watercolor markers
- Yellow and green colored pencils
- Small scissors
- Foam spacer tape
- Double-stick photo tape
- Envelope

1 Trim the cardstock to size with a paper trimmer or scissors. If you wish, use decorative-edge scissors to cut the white cardstock.

2 Color only the flower part of the stamp with red marker and stamp the scrap of cardstock. Ink the stamp with red and green markers and stamp the white cardstock. Color the images with colored pencils. Cut out the partial flower.

3 Attach the cardstock with the full flower to the front of the card with double-stick tape. Fasten the cutout flower over top of the full flower with foam spacer tape.

4 Open the card and stamp a bee flying across the card. Use a black marker to draw a dotted line for the bee's flight path. Then stamp one or two bees on the envelope.

Wrapping Paper

Handmade wrapping paper makes a gift even more special. You can make just enough for the gift you are wrapping. Or, you can stamp up a whole bunch and use it as you need it. Plan to use a large stamp. Otherwise this can become a very time-consuming project!

What You Need

- Roll of craft paper
- Pencil and eraser
- Pigment ink in three colors for background stamping
- Waterproof ink for image stamping
- Assorted birthday-themed stamps
- Blank business card
- Paper punch
- Metallic pen

1

Use the background stamp and pencil to mark a grid for the background stamps. Stamp the first background color in every third block of the grid to create a diagonal pattern.

2

Stamp the second background color to the right of every block you stamped in the first color. When you are finished, stamp the third ink color in all the remaining open spaces on the grid.

3

Using the birthday stamps, stamp an image in the center of each block of color. Rotate the stamp so the finished paper will look the same from all directions. Erase the pencil marks.

4

While the wrapping paper dries, make a matching gift tag from a blank business card. Use fabric ink to make a matching ribbon. Put paper under the ribbon to absorb the ink that seeps through it.

Canvas Beach Bag

Personalized canvas tote bags make great gifts. You can choose any theme at all. The theme can be related to what the bag will be used for. You can also choose a theme based simply on colors and images the person likes. The bag we show here is for toting beach gear, so we chose an ocean theme.

What You Need

- Blank canvas tote bag
- Scrap paper and scrap canvas
- Pencil and ruler
- Masking tape
- Alphabet stencil
- Fabric paint
- Paintbrush
- Craft or makeup sponges
- Beach-themed rubber stamps
- Disposable plates

1 Mark the border lines with strips of masking tape, using the edge of a ruler to tear the ends. Place your stamps and a cutout paper sample of the name on the bag to make sure there is enough room. If not, adjust your tape lines.

2 Stencil the name on the bag. Use a small paintbrush to dab paint onto the bag through the stencil. After painting each letter, carefully lift the stencil straight up. Clean both sides of the stencil after painting each letter. Paint the border lines.

3 Apply fabric paint to the center stamp. Stamp the scrap canvas. Press on the stamp for about 10 seconds so the canvas absorbs the paint. Decide whether you need to use more or less paint, then stamp the tote bag.

4 Prepare the paints for the border stamps. Again, practice on scrap fabric before stamping the tote bag. Let the paint dry overnight, then have an adult heat set the paint to make it permanent.

Homemade Stamps

Stamps you make yourself are inexpensive and unique.
In this chapter we'll show you three easy stamps to make.

Making a Sponge Stamp

Place your **template** over a pop-up sponge. Choose a shape that won't be hard to cut out. Shapes such as stars, hearts, suns, and moons work well. Trace the shape onto the sponge.

Cut out the shape with scissors. Then wet the sponge until it expands. Squeeze out the excess water before using the sponge.

To stamp with a sponge, put some paint on a disposable plate and spread it out with a brayer. Then just dip the sponge in the paint, and you're ready to stamp.

Making a String Stamp

1 Get a block of scrap lumber from your parents or ask for a scrap at the lumberyard. Draw a pattern on the wood. It doesn't have to be perfect. It's only a guide for gluing down the string.

2 Spread a thin layer of glue on the wood. Stick the string to the glue. If the string pops out of the wet glue, place a piece of waxed paper over the string. Set a book on top until the glue dries. Let the glue cure overnight.

3 Use a sponge to apply acrylic paint to the string. Don't apply too much paint. You want the texture of the string to show in the print. Now you're ready to stamp.

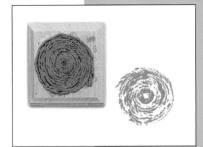

Stamping with a Leaf

1 Lay a fresh, soft leaf on a piece of scrap paper. The side with the raised veins should be faceup. Dip a sponge into acrylic paint and **pounce** off the excess. Dab a light coat of paint on the leaf.

2 Turn the leaf over and carefully position it on the paper. Press down on the stem while you slowly roll a brayer back and forth over the leaf. Put the brayer down, then lift the leaf off the paper.

3 To make a two-color print, reink the leaf with another color of paint and press it down over top of the first print you made.

Leaf Pile!

Apply paint to several leaves. Place the first leaf on the paper and rub gently. Without removing the first leaf, place the second leaf so it slightly overlaps the first. Rub gently. Add the third leaf. Rub gently. Carefully remove the leaves.

Glossary

commercial - artistic work designed to sell quickly and in large quantities.

detract - to decrease the impact or effectiveness of something.

embellish - to decorate. To make beautiful by adding decorations.

emboss - to raise the surface in a decorative manner.

eyelet - a small metal grommet, or ring, used to reinforce a small hole.

focal point - in decorating, the center of interest. The thing that draws the most attention.

impression - an image resulting from physical contact.

pigment - a substance that gives color to other materials. It is often a powder that is added to liquid.

pounce - in crafts, to apply with a straight up and down motion.

scribe - someone who writes for a living.

signet ring - a finger ring engraved with a monogram or seal. A signet is a mark used instead of a signature to sign a document.

solvent - a liquid that can dissolve another substance.

template - a pattern for making something.

Web Sites

To learn more about rubber stamping, visit ABDO Publishing Company on the World Wide Web at **www.abdopub.com**. Web sites about rubber stamping are featured on our Book Links page. These links are routinely monitored and updated to provide the most current information available.

Index